Great Football Stories

Football Babylon

RUSS WILLIAMS

Level 3

Retold by D'Arcy Adrian-Vallance and
Evadne Adrian-Vallance
Series Editors: Andy Hopkins and Jocelyn Potter

Pearson Education Limited
Edinburgh Gate, Harlow,
Essex CM20 2JE, England
and Associated Companies throughout the world.

ISBN 0 582 41670 1

First published in Great Britain by Virgin Publishing Ltd 1996
This adaptation first published by Penguin Books 1998
Published by Addison Wesley Longman Limited and Penguin Books Ltd. 1998
New edition first published 1999

Third impression 2000

Original copyright © Russ Williams 1960
Text copyright © D'Arcy Adrian-Vallance and Evadne Adrian-Vallance 1998
Photographs copyright © Colorsport 1998
All rights reserved

Typeset by Digital Type, London
Set in 11/14pt Bembo
Printed in Spain by Mateu Cromo, S. A. Pinto (Madrid)

Published by Pearson Education Limited in association with
Penguin Books Ltd, both companies being subsidiaries of Pearson Plc

For a complete list of the titles available in the Penguin Readers series please write to your local
Pearson Education office or to: Marketing Department, Penguin Longman Publishing,
5 Bentinck Street, London W1M 5RN.

Contents

Introduction

During a game in April 1962 one of the fans got really angry with the referee. The fan did not agree with something that the referee did, so he ran onto the pitch and killed the referee with a knife. Then another person watching the game shot the fan dead...

Football is the most popular sport in the world. It is played in over 200 countries by more than 117 million people, and is watched by millions more on television. The Brazilian footballer Pele was probably the greatest player of all time. He called it 'the beautiful game'.

But it is also a crazy game. It brings out strong feelings in both players and fans. 'Some people think that football is a question of life and death,' said Bill Shankly, the boss of the famous English football team Liverpool in the 1960s and 70s. 'But they're wrong. It's more important than that!'

In this book you'll read true stories about football from around the world. You'll read about the prince who tried to referee a World Cup match, the football games that started wars, the players and the fans who will do *anything* to win. Stories that you won't believe about the bad, crazy, dangerous, but often funny world of football – the beautiful game!

Russ Williams was thirty-three when he wrote this book. In this book he writes mostly about the bad side of football, but he loves the game. His favourite team is Spurs, a north London club.

He writes about football for newspapers and talks about it on TV. He also works for Virgin Radio in London. A second book of great football stories, *Football Babylon II*, came out in 1998.

Chapter 1   To Live and Die for Football

When I die, I'd like to die at a football game. I'd like to go quietly and easily, hearing the shouts of the crowd, smelling the smell of hamburgers. As I leave my body, I'll be above the crowd and above the pitch, and I'll see the game better than the television cameras can. There's just one problem: I'm never more than half lucky. So if I die at a football game, it will probably be just before the end of the game. I'll miss the last five minutes and I'll never know who won.

There are lots of people like me who can't live (or die) without football. For example, there is a true story about a Spanish fan. He was an old man and his favourite team was Real Betis. He went to every home game that they played. Just before he died, he spoke his last words to his son. He said that he wanted to continue going to the games after he was dead. The old man died, and the fire burned his body until almost nothing was left. A few days later his son went to the next game. He took a glass bottle with him. In the bottle there was almost nothing; just something grey, like dirty salt. People were surprised when the boy put the bottle very carefully next to him. Perhaps you want to know why the boy put his father in a glass bottle. Perhaps he wanted his father to be able to see out.

People have lived and died for football since the game began. But when did it begin? Nearly 2000 years ago, the Chinese writer Li Yu wrote about a game between two teams with a round ball and square goals. In about 1180, an English writer, William Fitz, also wrote about a ball game that many people played in England. He said that the game was so dangerous that it could be deadly for players and even for the people who were watching. The name of the game was football. At that time the

1

game had no rules. Any number of people could play, and the 'pitch' could be three or four kilometres long. There were always fights and many people were hurt.

By the 1600s, people were playing football all over England. The king and his government tried to stop it, church men spoke against it, but ordinary people loved it.

Slowly, over the next 200 years, football became less like a war and more like a game. By the end of the 1800s people were playing football all over the world, and the game had some rules. There were only a few rules, but this was the start of modern football. From this time, fewer people died on the football field, but modern football can still be dangerous.

Most football accidents happen when two players try to get the ball at the same time. That is how the famous young Scottish player, Jock Thompson, died in 1931. He was playing for the famous Scottish team, Celtic, in a game against another top Scottish team, Rangers. The ball was near Celtic's goal. A Rangers player, Sam English, tried to kick the ball. At the same time Jock Thompson tried to get his hands on it. He threw himself to the ground and got the ball just before Sam kicked it. But Jock's head took the kick. He died in hospital five hours later.

The next day thousands of Celtic fans started walking from Glasgow to Jock Thompson's home town. The walk took three days, and they slept in fields along the way. Football is so important to so many people in Scotland that even today Celtic fans often visit Jock Thompson's home town and the place where his body now lies.

Do you believe that people sometimes come back from the dead? People say that Jock Thompson comes back to the Celtic pitch where he played and died. Celtic now play at a new stadium. But if the story is true, there is still one player who comes to the old pitch every Saturday, hoping for a game.

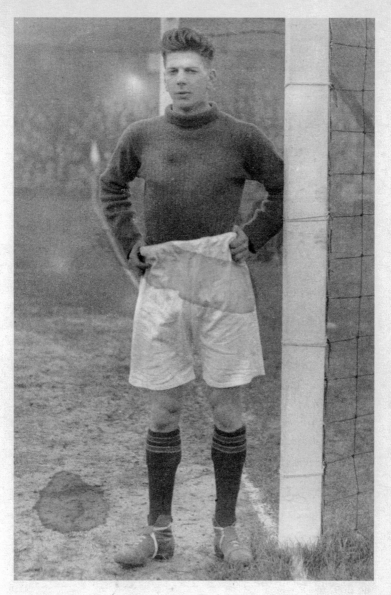

The famous young Scottish player, Jock Thompson.

During the two world wars football became less important. People did not have time to think about football then. In World War I (1914–18), there was no football in Britain. The government stopped it. But football brought the enemies together in a friendly way one Christmas Day in the middle of the war. That day some British and German soldiers put down their guns and played a game of football on the land between them, 'No Man's Land'. What a pity that they couldn't be so friendly every day of the year!

A few years after World War II (1939–45), some people died at a football match in a very strange way. The teams were playing in front of a crowd of 3,000 people. Suddenly a storm blew up. There was a loud CRASH and very bright light cut through the sky. The referee and eight of the players dropped to the ground. Most of the other players on the pitch stood for a moment before they fell to the ground too. Eight of the players went to hospital and two of them died. Later, most of the players said, 'It felt like something very heavy hit us on the back of the head.' Some of the people in the crowd were very frightened. They said later, 'It was terrible. There was this sudden light. It hit the referee, and he was the first to go down.' The referee was very lucky not to die.

South America is one place where it is always quite dangerous to work in football. During a game in April 1962 one of the fans got really angry with the referee. The fan did not agree with something that the referee did, so he ran onto the pitch and killed the referee with a knife. Then another person watching the game shot the fan dead. By this time, the crowd were very frightened. They were screaming, shouting and crying. They all started to run out of the stadium at the same time. One of them fell to the ground but the crowd didn't stop. They ran straight over him, and he died too.

At another game in South America, the referee gave a penalty to one team that the fans of the other team did not agree with. So they threw stones at the referee and killed him.

As we have heard, people sometimes see a person who died at a football game a long time before: a fan from the dead. But this seems to happen mostly in Britain. People say that there is a fan from the dead at Oldham's stadium. They call him 'Fred'. Fred was a fan who always stood in the same place at games there. He died in the middle of a game in the 1960s. Now people only see Fred early in the morning or late at night. The people who clean the club have seen him several times and they will not work there alone. One of the men at Oldham says, 'Fred frightens the people who clean here. He moves the things that they use for cleaning, and he seems to like pens too.' Once, Eileen, one of the women who clean, saw him in the kitchen. She was very frightened, but when she shouted his name, he disappeared.

Chapter 2   Fights

Football is a game that many people feel strongly about. Because of this, both players and fans often do things that are not sensible, things that they do not usually do. Some people say this sort of thing should not happen, but they forget how fast and exciting football is. People's bodies come close together. Things can happen in football which never happen in slower, calmer sports.

So, fights are an everyday part of football and probably always will be. The story of fights in football is an interesting one: it tells you something about people from different countries. In northern Europe, for example, there are very few violent or dangerous fights. People from Mediterranean countries like fights to look worse than they really are. In Africa, on the other hand,

People's bodies come close together. Things can happen in football which never happen in slower, calmer sports.

they can be really dangerous. But it is in South America that the most violent fights have always happened. Perhaps the past can explain the present. The great Argentinian writer, José Luis Borges, said, 'In the past, South Americans fought with knives; now they fight over a ball'!

There are many stories about things that have happened between South American players. Often these things start when the referee decides something that the players do not agree with. The players sometimes try to hit or hurt the referee and sometimes they tell the crowd to help them too. The referee in South America has a very dangerous job!

Sometimes it is the fans who start the trouble. For example, by 1916 Argentina and Uruguay were already famous for the terrible things that happened when they met on the pitch. At one match so many people bought tickets that the fans couldn't all get in to watch the game. So the teams were not able to play and the fans became very angry. They burnt down the stadium – the fire continued for four hours until almost nothing was left standing.

This sort of trouble has happened often. In 1964, 318 people died and 500 were hurt during a game between Peru and Argentina. Fighting started when the referee decided not to count one of Peru's goals. It became one of the worst fights in South American football.

It is bad enough when South American teams play, but if one of the team is from Italy it can be even worse. In 1969 the Italian team, AC Milan, played against Estudiantes de la Plata in Argentina. It was the World Club Final. When the players from AC Milan arrived in the country they did not get a friendly welcome. On the field things were even worse. The Argentine players decided to play violently and dirtily. They fought and hurt the Italians, and the referee did nothing to stop them. After the game President Ongania of Argentina felt that he had to do something about it, so he ordered two of the players to go to prison for 30 days. And they didn't play in the Argentinian team ever again.

There have been plenty of fights in British games, too. During the 1970s there was almost always trouble at important matches. The English football season usually begins each year with a match at Wembley. On 10 August 1974 this opening game of the season was between Leeds United and Liverpool. Most of the players were already quite famous. During the game the Leeds player, Johnny Giles, suddenly hit Liverpool's Kevin Keegan in

There have been plenty of fights in British games. This one is between players of the Manchester United and Newcastle United teams in 1997.

the face. Then he ran back into the crowd of other players. Nobody knew why he did it. When Keegan got up, Giles was ten metres away. But Billy Bremner, another Leeds player, was walking past Keegan. So Keegan tried to hit Bremner and quite naturally Bremner tried to stop him. It nearly became a serious fight, but the referee sent both players off. They did not make things any better when they threw their shirts down at the side of the pitch as they went, to show the referee what they thought of him. Johnny Giles, the man who started the fight, had a good laugh and enjoyed the rest of the game!

Some fights are more serious than this. In 1990 Yugoslavia was still one country and it was full of really good footballers. The war started in 1991 and Yugoslavia broke up into several smaller countries. But there was a lot of fighting before the war started, and one of the first serious fights was on a football field. Dinamo Zagreb, a team from one part of Yugoslavia (Croatia), were playing Red Star Belgrade, a team from another part (Serbia). They were playing in the city of Zagreb, the capital of Croatia. It was an important cup game. There was a lot of trouble already in Yugoslavia at that time and people were describing this game as Serbia against Croatia. Nobody realised how dangerous this was.

The match started with a violent fight between some of the fans. It was not the sort of fight that a few policemen could easily stop. The Serbs and Croats wanted to show how strong their feelings were. The police did not try to stop it – in fact they got into the fight too. The fans were fighting, the police were fighting, and finally the players started fighting too.

The Yugoslavian football league was one of the few things that still held the country together. A few days after this game the league came to an end. A few hours after that the real fighting of the Yugoslavian war of the 1990s began.

Football can bring people together or it can make things worse. During the 1990s some people planned matches as a way of helping countries. They thought: If these countries play a game of football together, maybe they will feel calmer and happier together!

The United Nations planned a match like this between two African countries, Ghana and Rwanda, in 1995. But the plan went badly wrong. The game in Kigali, Rwanda, ended in a big fight. One of the players was unhappy when the referee gave a penalty against his team, so he hit the referee. A person speaking for the United Nations said, 'When you put on a football shirt and tie up your boots, you leave behind any friendly feelings towards the country that you're playing against!'

Chapter 3   Frightening the Enemy

People sometimes try to get what they want by frightening other people or causing trouble. This happens a lot in football.

Sometimes it happens when managers and players shout angry things at the other team. Football crowds also love to tell the teams and fans of the opposite side what they think of them. But it can be much more serious than that. For example, at the time of the 1962 World Cup in Sweden, England's Jimmy Greaves said, 'There are some good players here playing very badly. They're afraid that if they keep the ball too long, somebody will kill them.'

This kind of thing has always been a part of football. In the 1880s fans often ran onto the pitch if they thought their team was losing. At the Scottish Cup Final in 1881, for example, Queen's Park were playing against Dumbarton. The Queen's Park fans ran onto the pitch so the Dumbarton players could not get to the ball, and Queen's Park scored an easy goal. The fans of the English team, Aston Villa, ran onto the pitch in 1888 and again in 1893.

Sometimes people even use the weather to make things difficult for the opposite team. This happened in 1928 when England played Spain in Madrid. Spain's manager knew how fast and hard the English team played, so he thought of a plan to slow them down: he chose a date in May for the game. May is often a very hot month in Spain. Of course this was more difficult for the English team than the Spanish team. The teams were at 3–3 when some Spanish fans ran onto the pitch too, and the English team lost heart – and lost the game.

In South America, criminals often kidnap famous football players so that they cannot play in matches. Or sometimes the criminals ask for something that they want. This happened in 1964 to a Spanish player, Alfredo Di Stefano.

At six o'clock one Saturday morning in Caracas, Venezuela, a group of men suddenly broke into Di Stefano's hotel room. They said, 'We're police! Come with us – we want to ask you some questions.' They hurried Di Stefano out of the hotel.

Several hours later a woman telephoned the hotel, the police and the Venezuelan newspapers. 'We've got Di Stefano,' she said. The criminals were in fact members of a Venezuelan group called the AFNL. The AFNL wanted to make Venezuela a freer place; they wanted to make things difficult for President Romulo Betancourt and his government. In a country like Venezuela, which eats and sleeps football, this was a perfect way to do it.

The government ordered every policeman to search for Di Stefano. But the AFNL kept him for 57 hours before they freed him near a Spanish government building in Caracas. They didn't hurt him, in fact they looked after him very well. But they used him and football to try and change their country and get something they wanted.

Giving the referee a hard time: Diego Maradona from Argentina did not agree with the referee during the World Cup semi-final in 1990.

People sometimes give the referee a hard time if he does something that they don't like. During 1964 there was a lot of trouble in football in Africa: in Gabon, Tunisia and Kenya crowds ran the referees off the pitches. In Kinshasa the capital of the Congo, the crowd threw stones at the referee and nearly killed him. In Zimbabwe, they had to close three stadiums for a long time because of trouble. Five minutes before the end of a game a referee had to run from one of these stadiums in order to stay alive.

About this time, in Zimbabwe, they found a new way to stop football trouble. The police watched the crowd carefully. If anyone was causing trouble, the police painted him with orange paint! After that it was easy to watch him!

Of course, teams and countries feel specially strongly about matches that get them into the World Cup. Winning these games is the most important thing in world sport. People say that football is a kind of war. In 1969 this idea came true – there really was war over a game before the next World Cup. It happened during three games between the teams of two Central American countries, Honduras and El Salvador. By the time the war ended 3,000 people were dead and 100,000 people had no homes.

The trouble started when the El Salvador team arrived on Saturday 7th June in the Honduran capital, Tegucigalpa. The first match was on the Sunday so the El Salvador players had only one night to rest and get ready. The Honduran fans wanted it to be a night to remember.

All night they made trouble outside the hotel of the El Salvador players. They made a lot of noise with their cars, threw stones at the windows, screamed and sang as loudly as possible. It was not surprising when El Salvador did not play as well as usual the next day. But the Hondurans only won by one goal.

In El Salvador the fans watching their team on television were not pleased. One eighteen-year-old girl, Amelia Bolanios, shot herself in the heart in front of her father as soon as the game ended.

A week later, the Honduran team arrived in San Salvador for the second game. A number of special cars took them to their hotel to keep them away from the screaming, angry crowd. But the crowd circled the hotel, shouting, breaking windows and throwing bad eggs and dead rats.

The next morning the cars returned to take the team to the game. Soldiers circled the pitch, and inside the circle other soldiers held machine guns.

El Salvador won the match easily, 3–0. The Honduran players went back to the airport, but the El Salvador fans started to fight the Honduran fans. They hurt large numbers of Hondurans and killed two of them. They burnt more than 150 Honduran cars. A few hours later it was impossible to cross from one country to the other. The problems between the two countries became worse and worse. The two governments had to try to do something about it.

The governments did not do very well. On the night before the third and last match they finally stopped talking about the problem because they were not able to agree. This only made things worse. They moved the match to Mexico City. The Honduran fans were on one side of the stadium and the El Salvador fans were on the other. Between them there were 5,000 Mexican police.

The game ended 3–2 to El Salvador who went on to the 1970 World Cup in Mexico. There was no real trouble after the last game but two weeks later the two countries were at war. It started when El Salvador's soldiers crossed into Honduras. The fighting went on for over four days. Finally the US government and other Central American countries talked to them and they stopped. No one won the war but football started it – people call it 'The Football War'. It was a pity that they were not able just to decide the problem with a penalty shoot-out.

Before the 1970 World Cup in Mexico, the English team went on a tour of Colombia. They stayed in the Colombian capital, Bogota. Two of England's most famous players of that time, Bobby Moore and Bobby Charlton, decided to have a look around the shops there. They went into a shop that sold silver and gold.

Later Moore and Charlton were sitting outside when someone came up to them and said, 'A £600 gold ring has just disappeared from this shop. Can you explain it?' Both men were surprised; they knew nothing about it. They didn't know that things like this can happen in Colombia. Moore and Charlton could not remember even looking at the ring. So they explained this to the police and thought no more about it.

The English team then travelled to Ecuador for a match. On their way back to Mexico for the World Cup they stopped in Colombia. The police immediately took Moore away and kept him in his hotel. The man who owned the gold and silver shop, the shop girl and one other mystery person all said, 'Moore is the man who stole the gold ring.' The world's newspapers and TV became interested now, because the English team had to leave Colombia for Mexico without Moore. Finally, the British government talked to the Colombian government about it. Moore paid some money and left Colombia to play in the World Cup.

People soon forgot the story about the ring. Nobody knew who started it. The mystery person disappeared. But the people who started it got what they wanted: they caused trouble and frightened the players. Maybe because of them, England lost 3–2 to West Germany.

In the Middle East people feel strongly about football, too: if the match is to decide who will play in the World Cup, they feel even more strongly about it. In late 1985 Iraq's most important sports newspaper wrote, 'If we lose, the fans will not stand there doing nothing. They will throw tomatoes and bottles at the losers'!

And a few years earlier, in the 1982 World Cup, a Kuwaiti prince walked onto the pitch and tried to take over the job of the referee.

Chapter 4   Scores: Honest or Not?

Sometimes people decide what the score is going to be before a game. Then they say to one team, 'We want you to lose', or 'We want you to score only one goal'. And these people pay the players money to get the final score that they want. This is a very bad side of football.

Most ordinary fans do not realize that it happens. They think that their team is good in every way, but this is not always true. People want to make money. There are always some people who will do anything to make money.

One story is about two of the most famous teams in English football. In 1915, Manchester United played against Liverpool. Liverpool were the better team but some of the players agreed the final score for the match in a pub two days before the game. The Liverpool players decided to lose on purpose. Then the players all put bets on Manchester to win.

In the game, Liverpool played very badly and Manchester won 2–0. The players won a lot of money from their bets. People realized that something was wrong and the police became interested. Finally, a Liverpool player told the police all about it. After that nine players had to leave the teams.

Liverpool players in 1915. They decided to lose their match against Manchester United on purpose. Then the players all put bets on Manchester to win.

In 1965 there were problems in both Yugoslavian and Italian football at the same time. It all started during one of the matches for the European Cup. The match was between a German team, Borussia Dortmund, and an Italian team, Inter Milan.

One of Milan's players, Luis Suarez, kicked Borussia's Kurrai right in front of the Yugoslavian referee, Tesanic. The referee didn't say anything to Suarez. The German players were very angry, but Tesanic told the players to go on playing. Milan won the match, 2–0. Later a Yugoslavian fan sent a letter to a Yugoslavian sports newspaper. The letter said, 'While I was watching a game in Italy, I realized, to my surprise, that one of our referees was not honest. In fact, I learned that the Milan team were paying for him to stay in Milan. They were also giving him money every day. What I want to know is this: if teams pay referees money, how can referees be honest during a game?' It was a good question.

When people read the letter, they were very angry: the referee in the letter was, of course, Mr Tesanic. After that he didn't referee any more matches for a long time.

Usually when people hand over money to change the score of a game, they use money that is *theirs*. But some people find other ways of getting the money that they need, and a bit more. The president of a Paris team, Saint Germain, thought of one way of doing this. He made two different groups of tickets for games. He sold one group in the usual way, but he sold the other group secretly. He didn't tell anyone about the money that he got from the tickets he sold secretly, and he used the money to pay people to get the scores that he wanted. After some time people realized what was happening. He was in big trouble and was soon out of the football world for ever.

There was one very funny game in South America in 1978. It was the Rio Grand Championships in the south of Brazil, and Gremio was playing against Juventude. Gremio had to lose because they didn't want to play a difficult match against Caxias the next day. So Gremio came onto the pitch, trying to lose! But after ten minutes one of their young players, Victor, scored and they were 1–0 up. Gremio's fans started to shout angrily at Victor for his 'mistake'. Then the referee, on purpose, gave a penalty against Gremio, which brought happy shouts from the Gremio fans. The score was now 1–1. But then another Gremio player, Ruverval, scored another goal for Gremio, making it 2–1!

In the second half of the game, Gremio tried to play as badly as possible and Juventude scored three times. A few minutes before the game finished, Gremio scored again just to please their fans. But their plan worked. They lost the match 4–3 but they won an easy way through to the next part of the Championships.

The game was so funny that people in Brazil laughed about it a lot. The manager of Gremio talked about it on television: it was true that his team lost on purpose. Of course, there was some trouble about it and everyone realized that it must not happen again.

In Italy, there was a lot of trouble in 1980. People were betting on the scores of games. In this way people made a lot of money. Before the game they paid the players, the players then scored the number of goals that the people were betting on. So the players made money and the people who were betting made money. People say that in one game between Lazio and AC Milan, someone paid the Lazio players £60,000 to lose the game. AC Milan won 2–1.

Sometimes criminals paid players to lose a game, but then the players did not lose. The players were pleased to take the money, but then they played as well as possible and won. This is a dangerous thing to do, of course. Other players, who took the criminals' money, made even more money from betting on the score.

Nobody was sure what was really happening, but then two men in the criminals' betting group talked to the police. They said, 'We've lost over £1 million because we paid these players to lose games. They took the money from us, but then they won the games!' The criminals gave the names of 27 players to the police. There was a lot of trouble and the Italian Football Association banned a large number of players from the game.

Of course, score-changing won't go away. It's something we are always going to hear about.

Chapter 5   Cheating

In the early days of football there were no rules, so cheating was impossible. But when rules came, so did cheating.

Sometimes cheating helped to make new rules. This happened in a game between the British teams Stoke and Aston Villa in 1891. In the 90th minute of the match the referee gave a penalty kick to Stoke. The Villa players knew that there was only one minute left, so their goalkeeper kicked the ball off the pitch. A Stoke player ran to get the ball, but it was too late for the penalty kick. Of course the Stoke team were very angry. After this, the Football Association (FA) changed the rules, so now if the play stops for a time during a game, the teams have to play that time at the end.

Some teams work really hard at cheating. An Argentinian team, Estudiantes, is one example from the 1960s. Juan Ramón

Aston Villa players in 1891. After their cheating in a game against Stoke that year, the Football Association (FA) changed the rules of football.

Verón, a player from that time, said, 'Before a game, we always tried to find information about the players in the other team – even about their families and girlfriends. Then we could say things to them and laugh at them and watch them get angry. When they got angry and tried to hit one of us, the referee sent them off.'

Sometimes cheats get into big trouble. At the Under 19s South American Championships in 1979 there was a storm of angry shouting because one of the Paraguayan players looked older than 19. In fact he was a lot older: he even had a four-year-old son. Two Chilean players were also too old. They changed the dates on their passports before the game, but they had to go home, too. When they returned to Chile, the police were waiting for them . . . and they went to prison. In 1987 the Under 16 team from Ghana had to leave the World Under 16 Championships in Canada because they had three over-age players.

Some of the top teams in Greece got into trouble in 1980 when they tried to use too many foreign players. The rules said that a team could have only two foreign players, but the Greek teams wanted more. So they gave Greek passports to some of their foreign players. It wasn't only the newspapers that were interested in this – the police were interested, too.

Some of the worst cheating was in Colombia in the 1980s. In that part of the world fans sometimes tried to kill referees, so some referees carried guns. Players used every kind of cheating, and their fans helped them. For example, when the ball got too near their team's goal, the fans didn't just watch, they often threw two or three more balls onto the pitch so the other team did not know which ball to kick.

Sometimes cheating is not so clear. Read this story about a team from Argentina and then decide: did they cheat or not? It was 1983. Sarsfield Velez were playing against Estudiantes. The first half of the game was not very exciting and there were no goals. But the exciting part was coming: during half-time the crowd heard four loud 'BANGS' that came from the Sarsfield Velez dressing-room. Then they saw smoke. One of the Sarsfield men ran from the dressing-room shouting, 'Someone threw something through the window! Some of the players are hurt!' He said the team could not come out to play the second half of the game.

Interestingly, nobody saw any of the hurt players. The Estudiantes fans wanted to see the players, but the Sarsfield Velez manager stopped them. In the end, the police arrived just as the Sarsfield Velez team were leaving. The police doctor wanted to see the hurt players, and they could not stop him. The doctor found only two players who said they were hurt. One player's eyes were a bit red, but there was nothing wrong with them. The other player said he couldn't hear anything, but he could answer all the doctor's questions!

The Argentinian FA had to decide what to do: the FA could give the game to Sarsfield Velez or they could tell the teams to play the second half another day. The important questions were: *Were the Sarsfield Velez players really hurt?* and *Did Estudiantes really try to hurt them?* In the end, the FA decided that Sarsfield Velez probably tried to cheat, so they had to play the second half. They played, and Estudiantes finally won 1–0.

There will always be some people who try to cheat, but Football Associations make sure that it does not happen too often. Some teams have paid heavily for cheating. One of them was the Italian team, AC Milan, in 1991. In that year they played against the French team, Marseille, in the European Cup. AC Milan were losing 1–0 when one of the lights over the pitch stopped working three minutes before the end of the game. The Milan players walked off the field saying they could not see because of bad light. This was clearly not true. They just wanted to be able to play the game again. The referee realized this and ordered them to return and finish the game. After that, the European FA (UEFA) banned them from European games for a year.

Chapter 6   Money for Players

Footballers have not always got money for playing. In 1884 the English FA banned Preston North End from the FA Cup because their manager paid the players. Their manager said, 'I have to pay them. If I don't, we won't be as good as other clubs. Other clubs pay their players, but they're just not so honest about it.' The same thing happened to another English team, Accrington Stanley, and after talking about it for a long time the FA agreed with the managers that they could pay their players.

In 1900, the most that players in England could get was £4 a week. This is like Paul Gascoigne getting only £200 a week today (he gets *thousands* of pounds a week). The players were not happy. They were famous people but they made the same money as the people who went to watch them! Because of this all kinds of trouble started. Of course, managers offered the players more than £4 – a lot more. And the players took it. The FA became very busy, trying to make things difficult for clubs that paid their players too much.

Today, when a player first starts playing with a club, the club pays the player some money. Sometimes this is a lot of money. But in the 1950s the most the club could pay was £10. The FA were very hard on clubs and players who did not keep to this rule. When Fulham's George Parsonage was starting with Chesterfield, he asked for £50. When the FA found out, he said, 'I didn't mean it. I was only being funny.' But the FA didn't think it was funny. They did the worst possible thing: they banned him from football forever. Until 1958 £10 was still the most a club could pay a new player.

Now, of course, players get much more money . . . and it is not only money. Manchester United were in trouble in 1980. The story was on television: Manchester United were paying the parents of boys who were still at school. These boys were very good at football, so Manchester United wanted the boys for their club. They even offered the boys' parents all kinds of expensive things for their homes. Manchester United is famous as the club that got Hugh McLenehan from Stockport County for three fridges full of ice cream!

Clubs pay hundreds of thousands of pounds now – and sometimes millions of pounds – to get the players they want. The rules of English football today are not against this, but they *are* still against paying money secretly or in a way that is not honest.

For example, in 1995 George Graham was Arsenal's manager. He was their best manager for years, but in February 1995 he lost his job with the club over money. A Norwegian agent, Rune Hauge, sold three players to Arsenal for more money than was usual. People said that he paid George Graham to help him do this.

Graham wrote a book about what happened. In his book he says, 'I met Hauge at the Park Lane Hotel in London. He came into the bar carrying a bag. We ordered a drink and he said, "I have something here for you, George." He opened the bag and brought out several envelopes. He said, "Please put these in your bag. Thank you for everything you have done to help me here in England." When I got home, I opened the envelopes. They were full of money. I took it to the bank immediately and the bank counted it. There was £140,500.'

Later Graham got another £285,000. He says, 'I took the money. Perhaps you think it wasn't honest, but it was only a

*George Graham was Arsenal's best manager for years, but in February
1995 he lost his job with the club over money.*

present. I didn't ask for it.' But he did not tell Arsenal about the money, either.

Then the newspapers got hold of the story. The FA and the International Football Association, FIFA, banned Graham and Hauge, and Graham had to give the money back to Arsenal. Graham says, 'The stupid thing is that I didn't need the money. I was just being greedy. If it happens to you, say No, No, No!'

Chapter 7   Girls

Everyone knows that football players like girls. And girls like nice, young football players. This often gets the players into trouble, specially when they travel to other countries.

Sometimes clubs use girls to get what they want from players and referees. This happened to one British referee, Howard King. It happened in games between top European teams. The clubs wanted King to make sure that the right teams won. In fact King never did what the clubs wanted, but he enjoyed spending time with the girls! The clubs could not say anything; they did not want to get into trouble.

Gary Speed was one British player who got into trouble because of girls. He was staying at a hotel before a game between Bolton and Leeds. One night he went back to his hotel with two girls. He was tired and fell asleep. The girls robbed Speed while he was sleeping. They stole his watch, his pocket telephone and £150. Of course, Speed had to tell the hotel manager, but he was not able to help the police much. He could not remember the girls' names or what they were wearing.

Speed's next problem was deciding what to tell his girlfriend at home. But in the end, he didn't have to decide. A Sunday newspaper, *The News of the World*, heard about the story. Speed's agent tried to keep the story out of the newspaper, but if there is an exciting story about a footballer and girls, it will always be in *The News of the World*.

There have been a lot of stories about the famous British player George Best over the years. Best was a wonderful player and he was also wonderful with women. The 1960s and 1970s were one long party for George Best.

A month after he left Manchester United, Best met Marjorie Wallace, who was Miss World. It started when she asked for a photograph of Best with her at a dance club in Manchester. As the club half-belonged to Best, of course he said 'yes'. He took her telephone number, and the next time he was in London he telephoned her. He arrived at her flat one Friday night and they went to some of Best's favourite London places. Then they spent some time together back at her flat. The next evening they did the same thing. But while Best was there, Marjorie's boyfriend's mother telephoned. When Best heard Marjorie's conversation, he became angry. The next day they went their different ways.

Marjorie Wallace was very angry. So she went to the police and said, 'Best has stolen some things from my flat.' The next Tuesday the police arrived at Best's dance club in Manchester. They took Best to London for questioning. While this was happening, the police got some information that was not good for Ms Wallace. There were some mistakes in her story and there were quite a few things in her past that she did not want other people to know. Because of this, Best walked free and Marjorie Wallace flew quickly to America.

Another time Best took a girl out to dinner. They sat down at a table with eight other girls. Then Best realized that he knew them all – they had all been girlfriends of his in the past! He just started laughing!

At one time Best even tried to get together with Brigitte

George Best in the 1970s. There have been a lot of stories about this famous British player over the years.

Bardot! He got her telephone number from a friend. But when he telephoned, he was only able to speak to the woman who helped in Bardot's house. She did not understand English, and she did not understand George!

Malcolm Allison is another player who is famous for a bit of girl trouble. He once arrived at a London football club, Crystal Palace, with a girl called Fiona Richmond. She was only wearing a thick winter coat, with nothing underneath. All the players wondered what Allison was doing with the girl there. They soon knew when they went to wash after playing some football. They all took their clothes off and got into a big bath as usual. But it was a surprise when Allison and the girl came in, and the girl took off her coat and got into the bath with them. Suddenly a photographer came in and started taking photographs of them all in the bath and, of course, these photographs were soon in a lot of the newspapers. Allison did not plan to make trouble; he just thought it was funny. But the wives of the players did not quite see it that way.

Chapter 8   Agents

Footballers need agents. An agent is a person who helps a player or a club to do business. The player or club pays the agent to help them. The rules of FIFA, the International Football Association, say that an agent can:

- Get any player for a club if the player is not already playing with another club.
- Agree with the club about the money that the club must pay the player.
- Generally do business for a player if the player asks him to.

In the past, there were no rules for football agents. They could do what they liked. But now an agent must be on FIFA's special list of agents, and he must not break FIFA's rules. If a player or club uses an agent who is not on FIFA's list, they will either have to pay FIFA a lot of money or FIFA will ban them from football.

Here is an example of what an agent does: Club X wants to sell player A to a British club. Club X tells the player's agent how much money it wants for the player. If Club X wants £1 million for player A, the agent will ask £1.2 million. The agent gets the extra £200,000 for his work and everyone is pleased.

In Britain agents often do more than this. They look after players in every way.

An agent once said, 'In Britain there are two types of agent – the ones on FIFA's list and Eric Hall.' This is true. Hall is not on the list and so some clubs will not do business with him. He uses the rules in a way that suits him. For example, Hall cannot talk to a club about the money a player wants, but he can tell the player's wife what to say. So he takes the wife with him to talk to the club. When the wife meets the people from the club, Hall cannot talk, but he can sit in the room and listen.

Hall is an interesting man. He wears strange clothes and smokes fat cigars. He says, 'I make the poor player rich and the rich player richer.' Other agents do not like Hall because he is not on FIFA's list. 'I love it all!' says Hall. 'They're frightened of me. But I've been in the business a long time. I think a player is able to decide for himself who he wants for his agent.' Perhaps this is true, but all businesses have rules. Is it right for football to be different?

If Eric Hall is one type of agent, then Phil and Jon Smith are the opposite. They have a company called First Artists. Football is the largest part of their business but they also work with English teams in other sports. People like the Smiths. They are pleasant and good at their job. They work with over 30 players and the Liverpool Football Club.

Some people think that working as a football agent is a wonderful life: meeting a lot of famous people and making a lot of money. But in fact the work is long and difficult, and you do not always get what you want. One story that shows this is about Joey Beauchamp's move from Oxford to West Ham. Phil Smith was the agent.

Everything was ready for Beauchamp to move to West Ham. The night before he moved, Phil Smith was waiting for Beauchamp. They were going to West Ham for an important visit. It was a surprise when Beauchamp phoned Smith. He said, 'I'm a bit busy, Phil. Can we go tomorrow instead of this evening?'

Because of Beauchamp, nothing happened for another two months. Then West Ham's manager, Billy Bonds, telephoned Smith. He still wanted Beauchamp. But Swindon Town were also interested in Beauchamp now. Bonds agreed to pay the same money as Swindon for Beauchamp.

Beauchamp liked the idea of Swindon, because it was nearer his home, but he agreed to move to West Ham. Eight people met in a hotel at Heathrow and finished all the business. West Ham paid £1 million for Beauchamp's move.

Everything went well. But the next afternoon Beauchamp phoned Smith and said, 'I've decided that I want to be with Swindon because it's a lot nearer home.' Smith said, 'That's not possible. Being with West Ham is wonderful for you. You're now in the Premier League.'

But Beauchamp was not happy at his new club and they weren't very happy with him either. He arrived late for matches and team meetings. He did not want to go on a tour to Scotland. If he had to go on tour, he wanted to go home every night! West Ham's fans began to realize how he felt and they did not like it. Finally, at one game against Southend, some of the fans started to hit Beauchamp. West Ham talked to Phil Smith again. Smith talked to Swindon. Swindon offered Beauchamp some money to move to their club. But even then Beauchamp couldn't decide! Finally he took the offer. But not long after, he went back to Oxford United!

An agent's job is not always easy.

Chapter 9   On Tour

One of the best things about being a footballer is going on tour. A tour is a trip to a number of different places, usually other countries, where the team plays against other teams. The players have a wonderful time and they enjoy telling stories and laughing about it for a long time after that.

Frank Worthington was a player for Leicester City. He remembers very happily a tour to the sunny island of Barbados, in the Caribbean, early in the 1970s. The Ipswich Town team also went on the tour. Before they left, someone asked all the players, 'Would you like to bring your wives?' The room stayed completely silent.

Of course, Worthington met a pretty girl on the island. He asked her to have a drink with him after a game. They enjoyed being together and they spent the next ten days eating, drinking, going to parties and having a good time together. Most of the other players from Leicester and Ipswich enjoyed themselves in the same way.

A few months later Ipswich was playing against Leicester City back in England. After the tour to Barbados, the Ipswich boys were worried. They didn't want their wives to hear about some of the things they did in the Caribbean. So one of them told

Frank Worthington was a player for Leicester City in the 1970s.

Worthington and the Leicester players to say nothing in front of their wives after the game. But one of the Leicester players liked to have a laugh. He walked into the room where all the players and their wives were with a big smile on his face. 'It was a *great* tour to Barbados, wasn't it,' he began. The faces of the Ipswich players suddenly went very white.

Players from the English team, Wimbledon, are famous for the strange things that they do to enjoy themselves on a tour. For example, when their driver is trying to park their bus, they sometimes offer to help him. But they tell him to drive the wrong way and then think it's funny if he drives into a wall.

On one tour to Germany, the Wimbledon players were staying in some buildings which soldiers used. Somebody said to them, ' If you hear the fire alarm, it means there's a fire, so please leave the building immediately.' The players had a plan, but they didn't tell one man, John Fashanu. They wanted to have a laugh.

In the middle of the night they all heard the fire alarm. Fashanu jumped out of bed and ran out of the building as fast as possible. The others got up slowly and looked out of the window. They watched him running up the road and laughed. Of course, there was no fire and it wasn't a real fire alarm. They were just playing a game!

On one tour in Bulgaria, Worthington met a pretty New York dancer who was staying in the same hotel as the English team. He wanted to spend some time alone with the girl, but an older woman was with her all the time, looking after her. So he asked some of the other players to help him. He wanted them to follow him when he went up to the dancer's room and take the older woman away somewhere.

He went upstairs and knocked on the door. The older woman opened the door and asked him to come in. But the dancer was not there. She was dancing in Paris, the woman said. Worthington

John Fashanu playing for Wimbledon in 1986. Wimbledon are famous for the strange things that they do to enjoy themselves on tour.

was not happy about this but he started talking to the older woman. She clearly liked him so he decided to spend the evening with her instead of the dancer. They were becoming a lot more friendly when suddenly he heard a loud noise outside the room. It was the other players. They ran in and quickly carried the woman out of the room and downstairs. They turned and smiled at Worthington but he was not smiling. Now he didn't have either the dancer or the woman to spend the evening with.

♦

As time goes by, there will be plenty more stories about the world of football like these – and probably much worse.

ACTIVITIES

Chapters 1–3

Before you read

1 Look at the picture on the front cover of this book. What has just happened, what is happening and what is going to happen? How do the three people feel, and why?

2 Find these words in your dictionary.

*fan   goal   league   manager   match   referee   score
stadium   violence*

Make *six* sentences. Use one piece of information from each box in each sentence.

They played	fans	a wonderful	the team
The	manager	started	violent
All football	the match	in	the match
The	referee	are sometimes	a league
He	clubs	belong to	goal
Football	scored	chooses	a stadium

3 Find these words in your dictionary.

kidnap   penalty   pitch

Which of them go in the following spaces?

a to play on a . . . . .   b to . . . . . a person   c to score a . . . . .

After you read

4 Make sentences. Put the information in the second and third part of each sentence with the right date.

a	In the 1600s	a player was kidnapped in	Scotland.
b	In 1916	a referee was killed in	Colombia.
c	In 1931	war started after a game between Serbia and	England.
d	In 1962	the Government tried to stop football in	South America.
e	In 1964	football fans burnt down a stadium in	Peru.

37

f In 1964   a famous player said he
wasn't a thief in   Venezuela.

g In 1970   318 people died during a game
between Argentina and   Croatia.

h In 1990   a player died from a kick in   South America.

5 Which teams are these sentences about?

  a A female fan shot herself.

  b They played three matches and went to war.

  c Their fans ran onto the pitch during a Cup Final.

  d The President ordered two of their players to prison.

  e One of their fans is dead but he still visits the stadium.

6 What did the Zimbabwe police do with violent fans? Why? Do you think this was a good idea or not? What other ways of stopping trouble at football matches can you think of?

Chapters 4–6

Before you read

7 Find these words in your dictionary.

  agent ban bets championship cheat

  Which of these words describe

  a something that you can win?

  b what dishonest players do?

  c someone who helps others to do business?

  d what football clubs do to troublemakers?

8 How can footballers *cheat* during a game? Which ways are the most serious, and why?

After you read

9 How were these people dishonest?

  a the Aston Villa goalkeeper   **d** 2 players from Chile

  b Colombian fans   **e** Estudiantes players

  c George Graham   **f** Mr Tesanic

  Which of these dishonest acts is the most serious, and why?

10 Do you think that footballers earn too much money now? Why, or why not?

Chapters 7–9

Before you read

11 Find the word *alarm* in your dictionary. Think of *three* different types of *alarm*.

12 These three chapters are about footballers, but not about football. Do you like to read about footballers even when they are not playing football? Why, or why not?

After you read

13 Which stories are these sentences about? Can you explain why?

  a Don't wake him up!   **d** That's not funny!

  b He's a thief!   **e** Go back to Oxford!

  c I'm sorry, she's busy.

14 Work in pairs. Act out this conversation between an Ipswich Town player and his wife.

  Student A: You're the player's wife. You are sure that he was with other girls when he went on tour to Barbados. Try to find out what really happened.

  Student B: You're the player. You don't want your wife to know about the bad things you did in Barbados.

Writing

15 Write a short story about a football game where something unusual happens. It can be a true story or fictional.

16 Describe your favourite player *or* your favourite team for a student magazine. Say why you like him/them, and talk about what they have done in the past.

17 Imagine that you have kidnapped a famous footballer. You will free him if your government changes some things about your country. Write a letter to a newspaper. Say why you have kidnapped the footballer. What do you want your government to do?

18 You are the referee of the *second* match between El Salvador and Honduras. (page 14). Write your match report. Talk about the police, the players and the fans. What are your suggestions for stopping the same type of trouble at the next match?